May, 2011

I wish you the best _____!
Let the journey begin _____.

Fondly,
Pattie 😊

Put Your Best Foot Forward

more little lessons for a happier world

Written by
Allison Stoutland

Illustrated by
Cathy Hofher

inch by inch
PUBLICATIONS

You don't have to see the whole staircase, just take the first step.

– Martin Luther King, Jr.

———————•———————

*REACH FOR THE SKY was our first step.
We could not be taking this second step if not for the great
support we've received along the way. We wish to acknowledge:
the many booksellers who believed that this small press deserved
a chance, especially Julia Caspary of Durham, NC and
Maryam Wasmund of Syracuse, NY; third and fourth graders
at Forest View Elementary School in Durham, NC who
enthusiastically "kid-tested" this book; as always, our
wonderful families; and especially the thousands and thousands
of readers who fell in love with REACH FOR THE SKY
and asked us for more...
thank you!*

Published by
INCH BY INCH PUBLICATIONS, LLC

www.inchbyinchbooks.com

Library of Congress Catalog Card Number: 00-101879
ISBN 0-9670941-1-9

To my mom
who gave me the foundation
on which to put my best foot forward,
and to my husband Jeff
for always being right by my side!
— a.j.s.

To my parents,
for always being wonderful
and supportive,
even when I wanted
to go to art school!
— c.h.

The sun
taught me...

to each new day!

to look forward

Ducks
taught me...

that it helps to look beneath the surface.

Apples
taught me...

that there is a star · within each of us.

Lions
taught me...

the power of my roar!

Puddles
taught me...

that you have to take chances.

Bunnies
taught me...

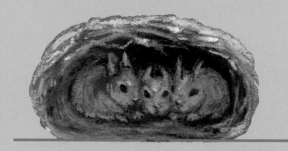

the importance of  listening.

Trees
taught me...

to stand tall and proud.

Eagles
taught me...

Sandcastles
taught me...

that my world is always changing.

Caterpillars taught me...

to put my best foot forward!

Mountains taught me...

that life has its ups · and its downs.

The moon
taught me...

that there is almost always a bright side.

Snails
taught me...

that home is where your heart is.